E-MAIL FROM THE SOUL
New & Selected Leadership Poems
William Ayot

I have witnessed first-hand the profound impact of William Ayot's poems on leaders seeking to take themselves to the next level. Through them, executives come to understand that they manage in prose, but lead in poetry. The poems in "E-mail from the Soul" speak — directly and intimately — to core challenges of leadership in times of profound transition. Michael Watkins, Author "The First 90 Days"

William Ayot's poems bring leaders face to face with a part of themselves many may have assumed was dead. Pain often follows the first shock of recognition, as they realise they had almost lost something precious to them. But with the pain, William's poetry allows us another discovery — there is life in our gardens that, with a little nourishment, could flourish again.
Narayan Pant, Director, Advanced Management Programme, INSEAD

William Ayot's poems don't offer comfort. They are tools for survival in an uncertain corporate world — a way to preserve in yourself, and to recognise in others, the roots of human feeling, passion, power and decency.
Philip Gross, Poet and Author, winner T.S.Eliot Prize

William Ayot's work is a wake up call to leaders. I have seen hard-edged engineers in senior management open their hearts in the face of his poetic wisdom. If you are a leader, or seek to become one; if you are in leadership development, or seek to be so, this book will be a treasured repository of provocation, balm and insight.
Richard Olivier, Director Olivier Mythodrama, author "Inspirational Leadership"

William Ayot's honest, hard-won and heartfelt poetry reminds us that timeless challenges can still find contemporary champions and that old virtues can find new venues, even — or perhaps especially — in the jargon-polluted corporate world.
Grahame Davies, Prizewinning Poet and Author

Occasionally a book comes along that changes the way we see the world and ourselves. For many of today's leaders I believe 'E-Mail from the Soul' will be such a book. It shines a spotlight of humanity into the heart of organisational life, and on the often unspoken, deeply felt, and kaleidoscopic path that leaders follow. A much needed gift to those who carry so much responsibility for all our futures.
Andrew White, Associate Dean, Executive Education, Saïd Business School, University of Oxford

also by William Ayot

Poetry

The Water Cage
Small Things that Matter
The Inheritance

Theatre

Bengal Lancer
Shakespeare's Ear

E-MAIL FROM THE SOUL

New & Selected Leadership Poems

William Ayot

Sleeping Mountain Press

© William Ayot 2012

Second Edition 2014 Published by Sleeping Mountain Press
Previously published in the UK in 2012 by PS Avalon
Sleeping Mountain Press
Courtyard House
Mathern
Chepstow
Monmouthshire
South Wales NP16 6HZ
www.williamayot.com

Design: Will Parfitt

Cover image – Nautilus & Skull – by Jenny Barron
Watercolour – From the author's collection

Back cover photo: Castle Portraits

ISBN 978-0-9930306-0-4

— To the Grandfathers —

Thanks
are due to the following individuals,
for inspiration, support and guidance:

Richard Olivier, Nicholas Janni, Michael Boyle,
Ben Walden, Yvette Forbes, Paula Healey,
Jacquie Drake, Mike Peckham, Neil Wooding,
Ludo Van der Heyden, Narayan Pant, Michael Watkins,
Otto Scharmer, Blandine Dupuis, Amanda Jones,
Ron Meeks, Andrew White, Yael Shazar,
Philip Gross, Dana Gioia, David Whyte,
Paul Groves, Ann Drysdale, Grahame Davies,
Juliet Grayson Ayot.

CONTENTS

A Foreword

Poetry and Leadership in the Labyrinth of Work

For many contemporary poets, there's something disturbing about a foreword in a collection of poems. One becomes suspicious. Should there be such a thing at all? Surely everything worth saying could have gone into the poetry? One also gets the distinct whiff of narcissism. Who does this guy think he is, Keats? As a consequence, poets tend to flick through any foreword and get to the poetry as quickly as possible....

But then this book wasn't actually written for poets. It was written for people who are often estranged from poetry, who might not trust it, who may have been baffled, or irritated, or even turned off by it. It was also written for those who spend the better part of their time guiding others through the labyrinth of working life. This book was written for leaders. With that in mind, this foreword can be seen as an introduction to the strange dance that poetry has been having with work, and leadership, over the last decade. It also points towards the internal journey begun by every leader who accepts their first promotion.

It seems odd to me that so little poetry is written about work. We spend millions of working hours in this strange land called the workplace, and yet the poetry of work would fill a very small bookcase. American poets such as Weldon Kees, David Ignatow, James Autry and Ted Kooser have written wry, touching and incisive poems about the details of managerial life. On this side of the Atlantic, with a few notable exceptions like Dennis O'Driscoll, Gavin Ewart, and U. A. Fanthorpe, work, and particularly leadership, seem to be something of a no-go area. Perhaps this has to do with the corralling of poets into the folds of academia and creative writing faculties, but the fact remains that, compared to other important areas of our lives, work and leadership rarely get the poetic attention they deserve.

This is even stranger when you consider how many of the great poets of the last century had considerable leadership experience. Statesmen, bank managers, insurance executives, lawyers, and publishers all covered the bases of public and private sector leadership, yet they turned out very little poetry about what Phillip Larkin called 'the toad called work'. There's a gap on our shelves.

I worked for over twenty-five years in London's gaming industry. Having also written plays for years, and burned out as both a dramatist and a casino Pit Boss, I plunged, or rather fell, into personal development. I spent some years, working with psychologists and storytellers, shamans and poets, addicts and therapists. For one deeply uncomfortable year, I even gave up all thought of writing. I sat and I listened, I watched and I waited. What came back was poetry.

Not long after this, I was asked by Richard Olivier to join him and Nicholas Janni in founding Olivier Mythodrama, a creative consultancy that uses story and poetry to explore leadership issues through the medium of Shakespearean myth and theatre practise. We were soon working for business schools and organisations at a surprisingly high level. Spending time with leaders and decision-makers, helping them to unpick their all too real dilemmas and paradoxes, I found a new and interesting field opening up before me. Adding my own feelings about leadership into the mix — I became a company director and chairman en route — I was soon writing for and about the people that I was meeting in seminars and coaching sessions around the world. I became intrigued by leaders: by the different ways they communicate and embody their ideas, the ways they operate, and the lives they lead.

These poems speak directly to the experience of leaders, to the men and women who, at different levels, lead the organisations that shape so much of our modern lives. As such they are rooted in the vocabulary, language and mindset of organisational life. I make no apology for this. Organisational language has it own dialects, energies and rhythms, as well as its deadening abstractions and clichés. Alongside the flat and avoidant business-speak beloved by managers — a use of language that George Orwell likened to a squid squirting ink — there is a clear and direct language of heart and imagination. We may mock organisational talk, with our buzzword bingo and superior sneers, but it's a fool who denies the medium he's swimming in.

The poems in this collection were often written on site, at business schools and corporate universities, during the away-days, seminars, workshops and leadership labs that I was leading or facilitating. Over the years, I became a kind of transient poet-in-residence: witnessing, observing, and writing up my experiences, then reading them back to the executives I worked with on that particular day. The Shakespearean references in this book are no mere affectation, they come out of my work with Olivier Mythodrama, which uses the stories of *Henry V*, *Julius Caesar* and *The Tempest*, amongst others, to illustrate and explore important points on the initiatory journeys that leaders undertake. References to Cassius, Brutus and Prospero are not there to score house-points, or to impress — they are merely allusions to the plays being explored and shouldn't get in the way of your understanding of the individual poems. That said, if you wanted to study leadership at its deepest and darkest, there is no better place to look than in the plays of Shakespeare.

Importantly, these poems were written to be spoken out loud. Having started out as a playwright, I have always written for the ear rather than for the page. This means that every poem in this collection has been 'road tested' — firstly by being spoken out loud, and secondly by being recited to a live audience of knowledgeable and sceptical executives.

There's something that happens to a poem and its reader when poetry is spoken. The resonant chambers of the body amplify and deepen the piece in question. New thoughts and old memories are opened up, depths and feelings reached. When you are alone with this book — or any book of poetry for that matter — you might like to read its poems out loud and see what happens, to both your understanding of the poem and your body.

If you read a poem to a group of attentive people, you can often notice an energy that passes from you to the audience and back again. It feeds both speaker and audience and, at its best, brings a gathering of disparate individuals to one of those deep and reflective communal stillnesses that the Quakers call companionable silence. It's a curious phenomenon, one which has exercised and engaged poets and performers from Taliesin to Tina Turner.

W.H. Auden famously said, "Poetry makes nothing happen". I disagree. In my experience, and especially in the highly focused world of modern business, a poem can serve as a wake-up call, prompt a long-overdue discussion, inspire a de-motivated team, or create a space for timely and vital reflection. Auden, who was watching his political dreams fade at the time, was memorialising another great poet, W.B. Yeats, when he wrote. The great Irishman, who was an activist, social entrepreneur and politician as well as one of the finest poets of the twentieth century, would probably have decked Auden for insulting his beloved art, or at the very least, told him to pull himself together. He knew that poetry could get things done.

If you've ever stood at the back of a hall when David Whyte was enthralling an audience of senior managers, or heard an executive challenging his company's attitude toward safety by reading out a poem about a corporate death, you would know that Auden got it seriously wrong. Poetry gives us direct, unmediated access to the 'invisibles', those unseen, unspoken qualities of empathy, imagination and creativity that give our lives both meaning and depth. It lifts us out of our left-brain obsessions with short-term, literal, reductionist results and mechanistic outcomes. More importantly perhaps, from a leader's perspective, it forces us to step back, broadening the narrow, unimaginative focus that bedevils modern business, the narrow obsessive focus that gave us Enron, Lehmann Bros and Collateralised Debt Obligations.

That fine poet, Dana Gioia, another successful executive in his own right and twice chairman of America's National Endowment for the Arts, once wrote a book called *Can Poetry Matter?* in which he made it abundantly clear that poetry not only matters, but that it must. He encouraged poets to get back into the broad public arena: to make our work more accessible, to link up with other arts, to engage new audiences, and to seek new fields of endeavour. A few poets, like me, responded to Dana Gioia's call by entering the field of organisational life and engaging with leaders and leadership. We are few but we have made a difference. Our poetry, prose and performances have helped leaders around the world to pause, reflect and occasionally re-think; to re-engage with their imaginations and refresh themselves on the journey of leadership. This slim volume represents my work in the field. I hope it speaks to you.

William Ayot
Mathern
2012

A Note on the Chapters

The Journey of Leadership

M any collections of poetry follow a thread that allows a theme to unfold and develop. *E-Mail from the Soul* is no exception. The thread of this collection follows an initiatory journey into, through and eventually beyond leadership, leaving us with a glimpse of a hopeful future.

Chapter One takes us over the threshold into the demanding world of leadership, challenging us to achievement, awareness and a kind of expansion — for in leadership we are called upon to grow in many different ways. In this chapter we also come across Middleham, a figure familiar to many of us as an also-ran, a colleague ill-fitted to the demands of top-flight leadership. His obsessions and failings parallel our own concerns, pointing him towards both disaster and later redemption.

Chapter Two invokes the gods in the garden, the muses of vision and language that alternately infuriate, baffle and inspire us on our journey. These poems explore the dry flat language of business-speak and hint at the depths of imagination and creativity that lie below. Like a vast and limitless resource they are there to be used on our journey.

Chapter Three reminds us that, like Ariadne, who helped Theseus to find his way out of the Labyrinth by giving him a ball of string, there are unexpected guides to be found along the way. We all have friends and allies whom we can depend upon, if only we can come to trust. At the same time, Middleham's seemingly nightmarish daydream shows us that we need to pay attention to inner guides and promptings too.

Chapters Four and Five transport us into areas of leadership where our own natures begin to shape events, where the inner voices that plague us can compromise our best endeavours. These experiences intensify as we find ourselves facing outside pressures and ever more searching questions. It comes as no surprise to see Middleham begin to flounder as he finds himself out of his depth. As harsh realities unfold, we find ourselves shedding our naivety and meeting something new in ourselves, a growing humanity. Joseph Campbell wrote, when referring to the archetypal quest to confront the Minotaur, "Where we thought to travel outwards, we shall come to the centre of our own existence; where we had thought to be alone, we shall be with all the world".

Chapter Six finds us in an oasis, a green space where we can pause and refresh ourselves before re-embarking on the deepening and broadening processes that John Keats used to call soul-making. This calm and quiet breathing space can have a profound effect upon us, opening us to 'the other', whatever that may be, in empowering and sustaining ways.

Many of us experience 360° Feedback as a helpful and valuable process of appraisal. However, we still occasionally experience a nagging doubt, that the superiors, peers and followers who fill out these questionnaires about us, may be holding back. Chapter Seven brings a septet of sonnets and other formal poems that show what each respondent really meant to say. These different views expose a shadowy side of Middleham's bullish and bullying nemesis, Ericsson. These dark capabilities — what Carl Gustav Jung dubbed the 'human shadow' — are a part of the human condition yet rarely acknowledged in the workplace until they explode with devastating results.

The poet Robert Bly once described the shadow as a black bag that stretches out behind us. This grungy old bag is stuffed with a lifetime's accretion of suppressed and rejected attitudes, behaviours, and feelings — all those things which were unacceptable to our carers when we were small. We can't see our own shadow because we are always facing forwards while the bag drags along behind us. However, those who love us can see our shadow, as can those who follow us. We all become acutely conscious of the leader's shadow.

Having seen the shadow at work in others, Chapter Eight casts a light on our own dark potentials, asking whether we are prepared to look at our own shadows, and at the shadows of our organisations. Jung, and later Bly, maintained that our task is to flush out those shadowy behaviours, to acknowledge them, and 'eat' them, re-absorb them as conscious parts of ourselves, not dangerous unconscious liabilities. As leaders, a failure to address our own and our organisation's shadows can have catastrophic consequences, as seen in the spectacular falls of people like Ken Lay, Jeff Skilling and Fred the Shred.

In Chapter Nine we find ourselves in that dark place where we can lose sight of the thread. Tested by loneliness, doubt and the repeated grazing that comes from the daily abrasions of leadership, we find ourselves in that most lonesome of places, where everyone is looking to us for an answer, and we might not have one. As much as we might wish to escape or deny, like Middleham, we are confronted by our own reality and the profound isolation of leadership.

'After the thunder and the rain', Chapter Ten brings us home, tired and bruised but re-forged and strengthened by experience. We now find ourselves in the garden of self-sustaining leadership, a place where we are able to care for ourselves, enrich our lives still further, and free the golden parts of ourselves we put aside on the way up the ladder. It is here, at last, that Middleham re-connects with his humanity, finding peace, and a kind of redemption.

Chapter Eleven finds us meeting age and the maturity of el-
derhood — not as a thing to be feared or shunned but as an
expected and grace-full part of the leader's journey. As we age,
both in and out of the workplace, we can feel disempowered,
but here we see the stirrings of possibility, and the richness of
the elder experience. Even the proximity of death need not
diminish us, for as we follow the thread of leadership through
to retirement and beyond, it takes a degree of age to truly ap-
preciate the sweetness of life.

Our short epilogue, Chapter Twelve, looks from the dusk of
age towards the future and sees a hopeful dawn embodied in a
young woman of infinite possibilities.

Acknowledgements

Many of the poems in this collection were written during events organised, delivered or hosted by the following organisations and educators:

Olivier Mythodrama, Oxford Saïd Business School,
Shakespeare's Globe, Columbia Business School,
INSEAD, The Work Foundation, Ashridge,
Cranfield University School of Management
(Praxis Centre), Lafarge University, Genesis Advisers,
Daimler Corporate Academy, London Business School,
The United Nations, AHRMIO, The Kings Fund,
Public Service Management Wales, Core Presence.

I

Crossing the Threshold

You Guys

For B W

             This is your time
For frosty mornings in towns you will never know,
For resentful receptionists and chirpy secretaries,
For flipcharts and outcomes, for plans and reports,
For too much coffee and too many words.
This is your time.
             This is your time
For dressing in the dark and cars to the airport,
For planes and trains and railway stations,
For loneliness, for grief, for embracing doubt,
For keeping hard secrets in the face of love.
This is your time.
             This is your time
For being what your people need you to be,
For managing fear while showing calm,
For being their mother, for being their father,
For holding the line, or the hope, or the dream.
This is your time.
             This is your time
For sudden sunlight breaking through the overcast,
For sweet green spaces in concrete canyons,
For the care of strangers, for anonymous gifts,
For learning to receive little acts of kindness.
This is your time.
             This is your time
For standing to be counted, for being yourself,
For becoming the sum and total of your life,
For finding courage, for finding your voice,
For leading, because you are needed now.
This is your time.

The Contract

A word from the led

And in the end we follow them —
not because we are paid,
not because we might see some advantage,
not because of the things they have accomplished,
not even because of the dreams they dream,
but simply because of who they are —
the man, the woman, the leader, the boss,
standing up there when the wave hits the rock,
passing out faith and confidence like life jackets,
knowing the currents, holding the doubts,
imagining the delights and terrors of every landfall:
captain, pirate, and parent by turns,
the bearer of our countless hopes and expectations.
We give them our trust. We give them our effort.
What we ask in return is that they stay true.

And This is the Deal

After Naomi Shihab Nye

Before you can call yourself a leader
you must come to understand failure,
embrace it like a sick, incurable friend
who looks at you in stark bewilderment.
You must see the edifice you created
crack and crumble, as in an earthquake;
witness the hurt and the disbelief, the shock
in the faces of those who trusted you;
feel their eyes on the back of your neck,
searing your skin as you drive away.

Before you put on the leader's coat,
you need to encounter your ruined rival,
see him stagger as he passes you by,
unheeding, rapt in the shame of his defeat.
You need to grasp that it could've been you,
sleepless, goaded by the need to win,
who crossed the line into recklessness
and lost a world on the turn of a card.

Before you know the lightness of leadership
you have to feel its suffocating weight,
to know that the sorrows of your people
are yours as much as the photos on your desk.
You have to plunge into the sea of their fear,
swim in the running tide of their anxieties —
dare to feel, dare to connect, dare to be
angry on their behalf — for until you have
shown them your tears and your weaknesses,
your power, like your kudos, remains a sham.

And then when the call to action comes,
when the e-mails fly and the questions get asked,
your people can show their hidden quality
by forming a hedge of trust around you.
Humanity, sown in time of quiet,
can reap hard work, long hours and loyalty.
The band of brothers can be a reality,
but the one who leads it has to be real.

Kuan — Contemplation

My friend in the bar is fulminating
against the iniquities of corporations.
He says they do bad things —
I have to agree with him. He says
they are formed for the purpose
of making indecent amounts of money,
and that, given the choice, a chief executive
is legally bound to consider his profit
before he considers the human cost.
I screw my face up and say, *You're right.*
He says all the corporate execs he's met
are hard, dry, boring, two-dimensional….
I say, *Now hold on a minute there, Jack!*
I've just been working with a bunch of guys….

And I think of the woman I overheard,
shielding her worried people, who fought
for them like a tigress fights for her cubs,
and the man who talked about his children
like a round-the-world yachtsman
far from home: the chief financial officer
with his yearnings and his abiding love,
the project manager with his scrupulous honesty,
the marketing genius with his humble heart,
the strategist with his quiet integrity —

and I think of the full moon climbing an oak tree
and twenty-odd people standing around a fire
and hopes and fears and decencies expressed
and I know that I'm proud to know these folk —
and I know that my friend has a lot to learn.

Why Should a Banker Read a Poem?

Because it might give him the lingering image
of a stick-thin, angry suburban mother,
bruised eyes blazing shock and bewilderment
as she sifts through the bits of her ruined life.

Because it might offer a couple of words
that jab him like a shaman at the very moment
of his initiation into a wounded maturity —
words like doubt and responsibility,
corollary, consequence and humility;
words that reflect how you choose to live
in a world that has seen you tumbling like Icarus:
helpless, humiliated, and disgraced
in a screaming welter of wax and feathers.

Because it can open him to the actual world,
tear down the walls of his secretive silo,
reintroduce him to old, forgotten loves
like a message in a bottle, washed up on the beach
of his five-star, barbed-wire protected resort.

Because it might show him a deeper wisdom
that lies in the art of doing nothing.

And at last because it might help him to see
that beyond the high-fives and the bonuses,
the pillories of shame and public contempt,
there lies a land of human possibility:
fed by the truth, not the fear of coming second,
rich in compassion as much as in cash,
a place still connected to the real and waiting earth,
a place where the famished heart can feed.

Middleham

Who is Middleham — and what does he want?
Why won't he tell us? He's ducking the question.

His thinning hair and expanding waistline
give us the picture of a company man, and yet

you wouldn't have a drink with Middleham.
Middleham's a singleton. He doesn't socialise.

He doesn't smile though his teeth are regular.
He scrubs up well and looks good in a suit.

He's always polite, acknowledges your e-mails,
is often the first to arrive for a meeting… and yet

you can never be sure that he's with you.
It appears that Middleham doesn't do empathy.

In psychometric tests and annual appraisals
you can sense his potential… and yet, and yet

his glass is always draining away. There's
something half-empty about Middleham.

Ericsson thinks he's a woolly thinker,
but then Ericsson thinks that all thinking's woolly.

Hopefully a transfer will sort him out —
Ericsson's convinced he can whip him into shape.

We wish him well, but expect some return.
We've invested a great deal in Middleham

Immortal

He tore round the corner,
judging it to the millimetre:
full-on, busy, impatient, and young;
expensive haircut, well-pressed suit,
blue shirt with just a hint of red in the tie.
I expected him to look clean through me
but he stopped, dead, in his inside tracks —
like a prince in a myth at a crossroads or a bridge,
when he meets the one-eyed, wizened dwarf.
We stood, each waiting for the other to speak,
strangers yet not unknown to each other.
It was as if he wanted something, and I had it to give.
The hunger in him was palpable; the hunger
of a man who needs some solitude, a drink,
a friend, or a damned good cry. We waited
as his hand gripped and re-gripped his briefcase,
knuckles whitening as he made a fist,
then relaxed, then made it again more tightly.
Finally, I broke the spell, saying, *Can I help you?*
No! he said and stepped around me. *No!*
and briskly walked away.
                              I watched him go,
watched the suit diminish, and cursed myself
for a fool. I shouldn't have said the 'H' word,
you see. I shouldn't have offered him help.
When I was like that, when I was immortal,
I couldn't have borne a kindness.

Workmen at Dawn

Five men, labourers, gathered at sunrise,
eating their breakfast on a concrete step.

The soft and delicate crunch of bread,
the tang of strong cheese in the mouth,

good food shared with one who has nothing,
tea from a Thermos steaming in the mug.

The older men smile at a youngster's bravado.
Their gentle laughter trembles the air.

The young man knows he will live forever.
The oldsters bask in the quiet of the day.

I want to say that this is a perfect morning,
that I am truly happy here, that I belong,

but I've yet to discover the facility of words
and, anyway, words are not currency here.

So I listen and wait, and try to stop smiling.
Let's go, says the foreman. *Let's get to work.*

News from the Plateau

The reports give measurements —
dates and numbers, times and distances,
heights and velocities; the age of the victim,
how far he fell, his years with the company,
and when and if he was certified.
They usually give a precise location,
with a two-line description of how he died:
whether he was married, how many children,
what he was doing at the time of the accident.

There's always a grainy, washed-out photo:
a windowless building site, a car in a ditch,
a forlorn and abandoned excavator,
its grab hanging empty like a crippled hand.
And always, always a little red cross
or a map with arrows for direction of travel;
the exact location of a corporate death.

But they never tell who held the hose
that washed away the blood of his friend;
nor how his mother covered her head
and howled at the passing of her only son.
They never recall the tsunami of feeling
that surges through the organisation:
the anger, the hurt, the withering shame,
the swell of grief, and the tide of sorrow
that comes with the news of another fatality.

The Hole

Everything begins and ends with the hole,
scraped as it was to ease the hip
of the very first hunter who slept away from home.

Rained on, enlarged, washed wider and deeper,
top soil eroded, bedrock exposed, the hole became
a gathering place, a pit of fires and midnight stars.

Nomads and wanderers rested by it; food was left
and gifts exchanged; gods were thanked; ancestors
gathered — spirits of place watched over the hole.

Stones were discovered in the dust: nodules of flint
to be flaked and chipped, grindstones and millstones,
rubble for walls. Men began to dig out the hole.

Great megaliths and temples have risen from here;
plain village churches and ascendant cathedrals.
Praise-songs and psalms have hymned the deepening.

Now dry, now dusty, now terraced, now sheer,
a deep and dirty crater grew, rang to the rhythm
of iron on rock, echoed to the work-songs of the driven.

Men have died to make the hole. Women have grown
and surrendered their sons, wept as it claimed
another sacrifice, another hopeful foreshortened life.

Limbs have shattered here, bones have snapped,
men have been ground into gravel and ashes,
their spirits compacted like fossils in the stone.

First it was the butchery of mattocks and axes,
then came steam and a terrible grinding,
explosions, and the scream of insatiable machinery.

Yet there was still a nobility here, the dignity
of honest labour, of skills acquired and handed on,
passed down by masters to their apprentices.

And in the quiet of the stone-built morgue, where
the uncomplaining corpses lay, men would bring
their broken friends, like gifts to place upon an altar.

This was the deal that was made in the hole:
that the need to grow and support a community
was balanced by the constant gift of blood,

first to the gentle spirits of place, then to the dreams
of the master-builders, now to the vision
of a global economy, the wider gathering of man.

So what is the contract we need to make now?
What is the gift that we need to give? If we live
for the numbers and the numbers are insatiable,
maybe we need to look into our hearts....

Getting There

Small stuff first: the paraphernalia,
the petty badges of wealth and success,
the watches, the pens, the telltale cuff-links,
no pinchbeck copies but the real thing,
solid and weighty to the knowing hand,
obvious to those who recognise the signs
of taste, reliability and worth,
the corporate lessons of understatement.

Then the suits, the rack of blues and greys,
the Prince of Wales and the bird's-eye checks,
the pinstripe serges and the subtle worsteds,
the cashmere-minks with their fold and fall.
Jermyn Street cuffs and cutaway collars,
monogrammed poplins and delicate voiles.
The hidden language of the cognoscenti;
never spelled out but the only way in,
the only true passport to the inner circle.

And the toys — the limousines and the planes,
the shine of woodwork and the smell of leather;
the nuances, gradations and fine distinctions
of business, first and executive class,
the tangible subtleties and infinite niceties
of visible success and ultimate arrival.

Later, when you get there, it doesn't matter.
The shares, the options and the fuck-you money
are taken for granted. You become entitled.
The things you craved on the way to the top
are almost irrelevant, unnecessary trifles.
Like the Buddhist's ladder you kick them away.

And when the stewardess greets you by name,
offers your complimentary glass of champagne,
you dismiss it with an air of practised ease.
Thank you, no. Could I just have some water.

Cathedral

Morning is stirring out in the suburbs
while down at Headquarters the building rises:
cleaned, dressed, polished and immaculate;
corporate marble awaiting the click
of well-heeled, focused decision makers.
The atrium creates a dynamic hush
of awed expectation, hope and ambition.
Elevators stretch and limber up,
their mirrors, veneers and ascendant buttons
shining in honour of reason and results.
Above, the chantries and clerestories
of reception, corridor and meeting room
already hum to the whirr of machines,
conversing with others half a world away;
tapping out the plainsong, the murmuring data,
the call and response of order and power.
Higher still, at the top of the tower,
in a teak-lined, austere, cloud-carpeted cell,
in the holy of holies where things are blessed
or cursed, confirmed or cast out,
there is a silence, a flat unimaginative silence,
the silence of exhaustion, cynicism, doubt.

E-mail from the Soul

For R K O

Somewhere downtown in the busy world,
amongst the siren-haunted high-rise,
there is a place or a time where something
tremendous is waiting to happen.
In a moment the over-carpeted world can change;
the walls you learned to lean against can give,
swing wide, to reveal a hidden landscape
of unimaginable promise — right there
amid the plans and the projected targets.

It is the call: the call that makes the MD quit,
that gets the Head of Systems into chaos.
It's a fax from the past, an e-mail
from the soul, an internal memo
from the psyche, or from God.
Sometimes it comes in a single headline flash
but more often than not it's in the detail,
the niggling detail that becomes a voice
which says, *I must change. I must change my life.*

And when it sounds — so clear and so terrible —
you're frozen with the fear of it.
Matthew sits dumbstruck, staring at his money,
afraid of the messenger with his prayerful hands.
And Paul, before that business trip to Damascus,
ignoring the voices in the ink and the olives;
Paul, the coldest of them all, driven to the point
where only blinding could make him stop;
even Paul, who changed the world, was afraid
and trembled because he knew the truth —
that in the end the call demands love.

II

The God in the Garden

The Night Ship

What do you want to do in this world?
What is your star, your far distant peak?
What dream lies unexplored within you
like a vast uncharted southern ocean:
daunting, demanding, compelling in the night
yet receding in the bright and busy light of day?

What discoveries invite you to the water?
What deck awaits your first excited step?
What ship, what clipper, what brave caravel,
what crowded ferry crosses back and forth
from dream to waking, dream to waking,
every morning of your undiscovered life?

Little Things We Call Upon

On a thick wet Tuesday morning
when the clouds hang heavy from the Peak
and the drift of incense from the Man Mo Temple
is lost to the stink of petrol fumes,
when the Star Ferry vanishes into the mist
and the blaze of Hong Kong side is no more
than a smudge on a wall of air and water,
when life is all questions and there are no answers,
and everyone's looking to you for something —
you have to dig deep.

That's when it arrives like the first notes of Schubert:
the demanding beauty of his *Die Winterreise* —
or a chord from Bach, or a theme by Mozart
so pure you could be listening to the voice of a god.
Maybe it's a memory of a time —
a time when everything was golden.
Maybe it's a word from a mentor, or a teacher,
or a movie, or an advert, or a line from a poem
that stuck in your mind when you needed something;
something to hold you, something to sustain you,
something to inspire you on a lost and foggy day.

The Idea

Even the coffee tastes good today.
Hunched over tables, leaning in,
excitement building in a rising circle —
excited looks, excited gestures,
grunts of approval, exclamations,
That's it... Like that... Spot-on... Exactly...
We've been working on that one too....
Laughter now, layered with delight,
connection colliding with coincidence,
synapses snapping to amazed attention,
everything informing the one idea.
And somewhere out there, a shapeless notion
waiting to be noticed, to be landed, pulled in —
the missing piece, the vital ingredient,
the essential component, Factor X.
In its own time it comes, arising naturally,
named just the once or merely inferred,
gathering itself with implosive momentum,
like demolition footage run in reverse:
a cloud of rubble unsettling itself,
bricks flying in from all directions,
forming, rising out of dusty chaos,
towering, complete and wholly new.
Then, the silence, the precious moment,
the circle of sparkling, enlivened eyes,
the unspoken praise in every smile,
the collective sigh that says, *This is it.*

The Diamond

On a good day, it sings.
It's more than just a job:
the calls and decisions,
the weeks of preparation
all come together
as sweetly as you'd hoped.
The tentative notion
you floated at that meeting
has evolved into an artefact,
an object to be proud of;
something natural yet crafted,
considered, cut and polished,
something solid,
your diamond,
something that will last.

How to Make a Bonfire

A smouldering at the edge of sight —
no more than a glimmer, the faintest glow.

Touch it. Treat it like a precious object.
Wrap it in fallen sycamore leaves.

Hold it, as you would an offering,
then bring it up to your lips, and blow.

Smell the quickening, hear the crackle,
feel the heat as the spark takes hold.

Now it's a flickering, a flame, a phoenix
dancing in your hands, a living fire.

Add it quickly to your old dry pile
of broken hopes and discarded desires.

Stand back now. You've created a fire.
This is how the future arrives.

A Doodle at the Edge

Another meeting, another agenda, another
list of buzz words, initials and initiatives.
PSU is entering Phase Three
while the CDR wants G2 to go to Level Five.

If we go the full nine yards on this one:
if we get proactive, get out of the box, get
our teams together and on the same hymn-sheet;
if we hit the ground running, if we downsize HR,
if we get the money on board, and our asses into gear,
then we can change something, make a difference,
change what the other guys changed last week.

Meanwhile the god has left the garden;
the muse lies minimised in the corner of our screens.
Not dead, not buried, but ignored and unseen,
like a doodle at the edge of an action plan.

Me? I say make a sacrifice to the doodle:
pick some flowers, speak a poem, feed the tiny muse.
Draw, paint, sing or dance, and you'll bring the gods
back into the boardroom: the laughing, smiling,
weeping gods of the night-time and the wild.

Company Metaphors

with apologies to Billy Collins

You could say that the firm is our meat and potatoes,
our plentiful table, our cornucopia.
It's the shining promontory on which we stand,
our far-distant beacon, our welcoming refuge.

It is also the book in which we are written,
the illuminated manuscript, the Sumerian clay,
the painted hand on the wall of the cave....
Well, maybe not the hand on the wall of the cave,
but I'm going with the book and the manuscript.

It definitely isn't the mist on the mountainside,
or the sparrow that flies in the mead-hall window.
And while we're about it, it's not a bowl of cherries.
Don't get me started on the bowl of cherries.

It may be that, once in a while, it's a bakery,
but it's certainly no rocket, nor a supertanker,
unless it's illegally dumping oil again,
in which case — Hell, let's call it a disaster.

At a push, I'll allow you a well-oiled machine,
but don't even think about us being an army.
That thing with the fighting and battling and killing;
you might as well put on a Nazi armband.

I could also do without the mushroom club —
I'm not in the dark and I don't buy the bullshit.
And as for the family thing, we all know families.
Remember the Barretts? What about the Borgias?

No, given the choice I'm an emigrating swallow
lined up and twittering on a telephone wire;
or a trawler atilt in a muddy harbour,
patiently waiting for the turning of the tide.

I suppose I could give you your cricket team,
though there's something juicy in a band of pilgrims.
But what about the outfit as a shoal of herrings,
or chickpeas on the boil, or a skein of wild geese?

In the end we'll always be bundles of images,
pictures to be known by, lived with, and grown.
One firm's bright dawn is another's Armageddon.
The thing about a metaphor is what it brings.

Above Lake Constance, Searching for Words

Our language is too debased a currency
to honour this run-down, radiant world.
Fabulous, as a word, is virtually meaningless,
at least in the mouth of an earnest exec
who is bent on *evolving impactful synergies*
to optimize bandwidth through gap analysis,
while *awesome*, when used to *push the envelope,*
or to *open portals to front-end deliverables,*
invokes all the awe of yesterday's porridge
or, worse, last year's impenetrable data.

The term 'fabulous' once called to mind
pearls on the turbans of oriental princes,
temples resounding to forgotten prayers,
languorous goddesses perfuming the night —
while awe should surely invoke the wondrous:
the awesome precision of a new-born's toe-nails,
the snowcapped Himalayas topping the clouds,
Venice arising through her veil of winter mist;

like now, sitting here, above the forest
spread out below me and beyond the lake,
rising in tiers towards the skyline,
dark and impenetrable, shorn of all context,
until, like a miracle, a single white water-bird
calmly and effortlessly describes a line
bringing trees and lake and sky together
to the muffled delight of distant bells.

III

A Gift of String

The Heroes of Everyday Life

No great discoveries, no leaping eureka moments,
no vast overarching schemes or achievements,
but the daily rituals of getting on:
the school run, the gym, the drive to the office;
a kind word here, some friction there,
maybe some rivalry, a hint of an edge.
Queuing for lunch and counting the calories,
shop-talk that eats up the precious hour;
meetings and calls, the occasional trip —
the promise of adventure, the sniff of romance
though home as usual with presents and a sigh
to the midnight tenderness of kissing sleeping heads.
These are the heroes of everyday life,
neither visionary nor driven, but reliable, steady,
with curbed desires and attainable goals:
the house, the holiday, the golf club, the car;
the yearnings, the hungers, and the ache for a purpose.
They're our friends and acquaintances, husbands and wives.
They are parents, consumers, the pillars of the world.
They are the audience. They are the led.
What do we know of their silent sacrifices?
What can we know of their unspoken dreams?

Ariadne: A Little Poem About Gratitude

I was the one in the green leather chair
that rainy day at your first presentation,
the one who gave you the welcoming smile
which helped you over your newcomer's nerves;
who passed the note that gave you an answer,
who told the others you had potential.

And it was I who opened your office door
that morning you failed the interview;
who saw you staring at the calendar, shaking
as you realised you'd burned your platform;
who bucked you up and spared you sympathy,
who showed you ways to be indispensable.

Mine was the hand resting on your arm
with a quiet steer and a tender word,
the gentle laugh holding your attention,
curbing the flight of your young falcon —
who whispered when your thoughts were diving,
Not now. Not now. This too will pass.

And I was the one you made the joke about
when you were buzzing after the road show;
the one who was useless and over the hill,
who came up short, who didn't matter.
And I was the one you never got round to,
the Christmas card you always forgot.

At the Edge of the Village

'Mad as a fish and twice as slippery',
she doesn't fit, and knows it.
The comments from her workmates hurt her,
but they're meant to. She's a weirdo.
She scares them with her clumsy kindness,
her open-hearted way of offering,
while the tribal mask of her great gawpy face
with its car-crash make-up and wobbly lip
does nothing to render her more appealing
to young men looking for an opportune bonk,
or girls who need a talkative mirror
to assure them of their bloom and loveliness,
the inevitability of their pulling a prince.

In another time there would have been a place,
a cottage in a wood at the edge of the village
with mildewed thatch and a threadbare hen
pecking at nothings on a hard earth floor;
a place where a man might come by a charm,
or the answer to a dream, or a poultice for a wound;
where a girl who had nowhere else to go
could ask for a draft to rid her of her shame,
or a herb to add lustre to the glory of her hair;
a place where an elder might appear after dark
to ask for a potion which he greedily took
but never acknowledged in the light of day,
a potion which would bind them to a risky silence
and a debt which he hated and would never repay.

No place then, no welcome, no belonging,
not even the sharing of a biscuit on a break;
just a lopsided smile and a looming presence,
an awkward offer to read a worried palm.

Middleham's Daydream

In his reverie, in quest of daily bread,
through chilling porticos of polished stone,
the pink-faced men of granite, hooked on risk,
seek out their high before the coming low,
the cleansing low that washes all away.

A warning bell is rung, panic sets in,
and in the sudden rush to raise high ground
Middleham stumbles. Maybe he is pushed.
Yes, he's pushed. Water closes over him.
Some say drowning holds a kind of comfort
if you can let go — and he finds he can,
helped as he is by the heel of a friend
crushing his hand till it loses its grip.

It's easier than he thought. No sooner down
than out, no sooner out than floating free;
free of the house, the car, the two-fifty thou'
and all the hard-won toys that meant so much
before he broke them or the batteries went flat.

So, swirling and turning, floundering down,
he's brought to the very base of the cliff
where in the living rock he sees a child,
suspended, held, enambered like a fly,
serene and sightless in a crystal womb
lit by the past and strangely familiar.
Middleham knows he's drowning in sadness.
He reaches out, to touch and to remember.

Personal Assistant

Sometimes he talks to me about progress,
about how the coming times
will bring about a change in people,
about how mankind will step up
over the dry white bones of history
to make the world a perfect place
and man himself a paragon.
                              I look at him then:
the deep conviction, the wild and messianic glitter
of one whose ambition has married his certainty.
I bite my tongue and get on with my work.
Sometimes he tries to improve on things,
to arrive at perfection through answers and remedies,
solutions to mysteries that he calls problems.
I don't say anything — it's not my place —
but it's hard to watch him at times like that:
ferociously concentrated, intent yet ensnared,
turning on himself like a fox in a gin-trap,
tearing at everything, even himself,
for the sake of a freedom he could never enjoy.
I want to say, *Stop it, you're hurting yourself,*
like you would to a child who knows no better.
And sometimes I want to hold him —
to comfort or crush the craziness out of him —
but still I say nothing. I keep my peace.
He's not the kind of boss you can talk to.

What Got Things Done

In the fire's glow what we remember
is not the size or weight of the pay cheque,
the power we rode like a bolting stallion,
nor even the plaudits and the accolades,
but what we made and who we made it with —
that one sweet thing we built together.
And what we recall, when the data's long shredded,
are the faces of those we loved in the making.

Like a craftsman at his bench who studies his mate,
or the master whose eyes alight on his apprentice,
we soften at the memory of particular faces
that in our work felt closer than our families.
These were the ones who forged us a fellowship,
the work-roughened, busy, and committed few
who subsumed their dreams in our desires
and gave themselves to further our ambition.
At times we forgot them, wilfully ignored them,
took them for granted, or pushed them too far,
until we were touched by a tender silence,
a quiet withdrawal, or a hand upon our sleeve.

Even the ones who broke away and left us,
who showed us ourselves in the midnight mirror;
the ones who weathered our scorn and distrust,
who, leaving, were doused in our disappointment.
Even they hold a place in our tired hearts
and gather as we gaze at the late fire's embers.
Looking back, we know what got things done.
It was just that, at work, we could never name it.

IV

Entering the Field

The Giant's Gold

When you were young, still fresh from the egg,
when the world of work opened up before you
like a path through a strange mythological landscape
with its castles and dragons guarding pots of gold,
there was a giant who lived at the top of a tower,
a fearsome creature you saw now and then
who roared and demanded and shook the ground,
whose every move you tracked and anticipated,
scared yet hoping to be seen. Sometimes you met
in unlikely places. Turning a corner you were surprised,
trapped and confronted, breathless and gawping,
face to face with an ogre, and alone.

What happens then makes all the difference:
an interested question, a genuine smile.
The kindness of giants makes heroes of bumpkins,
princesses of maids and kings out of boys.

So what do you do, when you bump into a greenhorn?
Do you bless with a moment of your precious time,
or curse with an absence, a frowning dismissal
that crushes young hope like a boot on a flower?

This is your treasure, your greatest offering,
your magical, reforged and sacred sword —
and this is the moment you pass it on
like a torch or a banner or a whispered dream.
Your time is your gift. It changes people.
It can give new direction, or light a flame.
So, when you see that kid in the corridor,
bashful and clumsy and longing for a word,
remember your power to curse or bless.
The choice is yours. You are now the giant.

His Liberal Eye

From the car to the door is forty metres,
reception to the elevator twenty-five more.
Eighteen floors up and another thirty paces
down a carpeted corridor to a panelled room.

Every step brings a small interaction,
a smile or a word for everyone he sees:
a child in hospital, a graduation,
some football banter, a moment for a loss.

This is no performance, this is breaking bread,
the daily sacrament of being seen;
of greeting, blessing, spreading one's presence,
of bestowing the gift of the boss's time.

The slightest lapse here, the smallest gesture:
a frown, a grimace, a worried look,
would carry the weight of a malediction.
Great ships can sink for want of a smile.

Alone in his office, he gets down to business
as invisible messages move out into the world.
The captain was smiling. We're on course.
All can be well. It can be a good day

A Secret Language

In the room, it matters who you are.
The old way of doing things, that got you here,
no longer serves you. It's about power.

Subtleties matter here. Every move you make:
every nod, every frown, every casual gesture,
sends messages, rippling out into the morning.

Those impatient fingers tapping the table,
the wringing of your hands, that glance
at your watch, might just as well be neon signs
announcing each shift of mood or intention.

And under the table, your restless feet, so keen
to move on, to get to an outcome, are making
signals of a different kind — saying look,
it's just me. You don't have to take me seriously.

This is the unspoken language of power,
clear and precise with its own fixed grammar,
its particular usage and vocabulary,
its way of placing you exactly where you are.

There is no phrase book. You're on your own.
Your only guide is your practised attention.
Inside you is the wisdom of the watching child,
and the deep, dark learning of a million years.

Present

Not back then,
not in the vigilant, demanding past
with its rules and drivers,
its hard-won certainties,
its logical, reasonable, learned imperatives.

Not in the future
in plans or expectations,
in shining, aspirational goals and outcomes;
in long-held desires that arc towards horizons —
like comets that lift us out of ourselves,
trailing the fiery wreckage
of innumerable unlived experiences.

But now in the simple, humble moment
with its truth and solidity, its authenticity,
its relaxed, committed yet unforced attendance:
alert yet calm, confident yet open,
the living paradox of being present.
Not a story but an epiphany,
not a journey but an arrival,
not a path but a field, widening and widening.
Never more singular. Ever more connected.

Fools and Imposters

It makes you wonder how anything gets done.
So many voices telling us we're crap.

Take the shy little man with the ill-fitting suit
who turned a run-down paper factory
into a major multinational, in spite
of the pitiless inner voices saying,
Fool! Who are you to succeed? Imposter!

Or the sad-eyed woman who studied nights
to become a lawyer, while she brought up
two kids and held down the day job, haunted
by the words of her father telling her
she'd never amount to anything. Worthless…

Or maybe the swaggering East End wide boy
who turned a barrow into a high-street giant
while, in his head, his teacher's malediction
nailed him forever to the bottom of the class.

Sometimes I'm minded of all the others,
the ones whom the voices mugged and defeated,
the ones who never had a chance — punished
for imagining they might be different, curbed
and restricted, beaten down, crucified.

We're all of us stupid, none of us good enough,
the voices tell us so every day — unbelievable,
liars and idiots, fools and imposters every one.

Middleham and the Voices

And there they all are, hanging in the air,
jeering like a bunch of drunken gangsters,
loitering with intent to mug and shame you,
poisonous, cruel, fizzing with venom,
so well rehearsed they've become a part of you.
Every stuttering halt and toxic silence,
every dry-mouthed, stumbling presentation,
gives them more power, pays them protection,
sees them strutting their puffed-up stuff.
They gloat, they pose, they smoke their cigars,
they wear their tasteless look-at-me suits,
and all the while you are shrinking, dwindling,
shrivelling as failure adheres to failure.

Coming to Bless

Rachel at Reception, always helpful,
Gina in Catering, gentle and kind,
Jo from Finance, bruised and indignant,
needing to know that she still belongs;

George the junior, so keen, so up for it,
perennially perky and full of ideas;
and Meera from Sales, Meera the Martyr,
holding things together in spite of it all.

Often it's a simple confirmation,
a joke to be shared, however lame.
Sometimes we can stop to see a photo,
to make a connection, even with a frown.

Norman's lugubrious as a bloodhound
— he's seen it all before and seen it sour —
while bashful Asif is full to bursting,
needing just a moment to tell of his son.

These are the faces that greet us daily,
the hopeful, the needy, the sad, and the raw.
Ignore them, and we lose our humanity:
welcome them, and we heal the world.

V

The Belly of the Whale

On Being an Englishman and Having a Nice Day

An American woman calls me at the crack of dawn.
She wants me to know how disorganised I am.
I already know this but she needs to tell me anyway.
She says, *You're disorganised.* I say, *Yes.* She says,
I've never known such a disorganised organisation.
I don't say anything much but I think three things:
firstly, she's right; and secondly, she's never lived;
thirdly, I think this woman's beginning to piss me off.
I don't feel anything, except that I note a small shift
inside me, like a tiny ember tumbling in a grate.
Then, as she continues to pass me under the harrow,
I close down. I go numb. The blood leaves my skin,
my hands go cold, and, as her voice moves up another
octave, I find myself wondering what it would be like
to put my hands around her throat and strangle her.
She's getting into her stride now, and so am I.
As she itemises my failings, one by one, I get her
down on the floor and throttle her, along with
my mother, and a gaggle of would-be-mother clones.
Finally she stops and says something American about
making this a 'learning experience', which comes
across in English as, 'Let that be a lesson to you,
my man'. I wipe the telltale spittle from my mouth
and whisper, *Thank you, madam. Have a nice day.*

The Chosen One

They give you precisely one hour, over lunch.
They control themselves. They give nothing away.
They know just how long to spend on each topic:
how long to sound wistful about holidays or golf,
and exactly when to offer you the bejewelled
dagger of duplicity.
              They place it, gingerly,
on the linen cloth, between the bread and the salt,
where it catches the light as the talk moves on
to your progress and future within the organisation.

Doing what they want means risking everything
because everything said will be unattributable.
You know it. They know it. Everybody knows it.
Everybody knows you'll be on your own.
                      Coffee,
and the dagger is nudged an inch towards you.
Nothing is said, but while they sign for the bill
you are expected to pick up the dagger, to say
yes to the deed, like an acolyte of the Assassins,
like the chosen one whose time has come to move
out into the darkness.
             In the fifty-ninth minute
they have to dash. Their parting handshake is firm
and brisk; their eyes are clear and full of meaning.
You stay on afterwards, in the empty restaurant,
staring at the blade and the jewel-encrusted handle.
You ponder fine notions like integrity and loyalty
but they mean nothing when weighed against words
like mortgage, and family, and the kids' education.
When you reach out your hand — as you know
you must — you notice you're no longer shaking.

Downturn

Now it begins —
the slow withdrawal into ourselves,
the shutting down of care and connection,
the thoughtless slights and petty cruelties
that mark the arrival of another recession.

Finally the word itself is spoken:
held back for the winter, denied all spring,
quarter after quarter of increasing pressure,
forming itself in the mouths of executives,
blurted by managers too young to remember.

At first, like a subtle shift in the weather,
it shows itself in a drizzle of language,
in dull and dreary, mean-spirited euphemisms;
in downsizing, outplacement, and rationalisation.
Then, as the cold front of scarcity develops,
the shorter, more brutal words appear:
words like shut, stop, sale, and strike;
cutback, crisis, closure, and the sack.

Only later does the damage become visible:
the red-rimmed eyes of a foreman, forsaken
by the figures and the harsh realities of value;
fifty-year-old managers, dressing like teenagers,
proving themselves by betraying old friends;
the casual woundings of direct reports,
the hard word, delivered as an act of revenge.

I remember the faces of colleagues
haunted by their failure to house the family;
women pinched or blowsy with despair,
waiting in line for the cold slap of charity;

children like ghosts from leather-bound novels
relearning the hatreds of privilege and caste,
their eyes accusing, even as they begged
for attention, or the price of a bottle of cider.

I want us to think where we might be going
and consider our choices in whatever comes.
To hide behind the numbers is a cop-out.
We are kindred, gathered at the edge of a storm.

Going Forward

One day the CEO arrived,
asked Phil Murphy for three key words
that captured where we were as a division,
and set up an impromptu road show in the canteen.
He wore a cream voile shirt and crocodile shoes,
a California tan and a suit that could blind you.
He talked for over half an hour, extemporised
on Phil's three words, which were:
Marketing, Service, and *Integrity*.
As he dazzled us all with his style and rhetoric
Phil looked over his shoulder and beamed at us.
Isn't this great, he said. *This is leadership!*

Later, it became clear that the CEO was a crook,
or at least a fox who'd lucked into a fortune
and then got out before the whole thing collapsed.
Phil stayed on, though he aged twenty years,
as he managed what they called the restructuring.
He made cuts, deep cuts, and he made decisions:
sacked old friends and kids he'd encouraged.
He took all the anger, absorbed the resentment,
his hair going white as he did what was needed
to save, and survive, to keep things going.

When the worst was over, and the shares
were recovering, with his stakeholders happy
and the market buzzing, the new CEO paid us a visit.
He was different, contained, full of quiet certitude,
and he didn't talk much, being a man of few words,
but he did tell Phil he had an hour to clear his office.
You're finished, he said. *It's key... going forward.*

They got Phil a taxi, because they kept his car,
so he had to sit alone in reception:
shunned and avoided, stared at and humiliated,
his working life reduced to an archive box
balanced on his lap as he stared straight ahead.

A Change of Culture

Everything happens very quickly.
The job, the car, the friends, the dream:
all vanish overnight.
Suddenly you're going down the pipe,
a nobody with nothing,
and nothing to look forward to.

You become a social security number,
shuffling shoes in an endless queue,
a little bag of memories, spilled out
in vain across a pawnbroker's mat,
sifted, sorted, priced and rejected.
You learn to lie — they expect you to.

One of us becomes one of them,
a transparent man with an arrogant step,
a jaunty smile and a haunted look,
the type you used to follow like a sniper,
picking them off with distant pity.
You learn to hate — selectively.

And then one evening, by the river,
your pockets stuffed with final demands,
you look at the skyline and see a sunset
so finely washed you catch your breath.
Sensing a delicate change in the seasons
you savour the world, and you are opened.
You wander home, trembling and amazed,
exhalting in a sudden awareness.
You kiss your wife as if for the first time
and later that night you wait up,
watching over her. When the tears come
at last, they feel wholesome and clean.

Still

They say that the first one is the hardest
and that it gets easier.
                    Well, it doesn't.
They still come in with that look on their face,
flash their tired smile, and sit there waiting.
They still expect you to do all the work,
to flush them out with the same old questions,
and their lies are still as transparent as ever.
They just didn't know. It wasn't their fault.
You couldn't expect them to see it coming.
And when you push, you still feel the give,
the soft withdrawal into wounded silence.
But it was your job, your responsibility.
Why didn't you say while there was still time?
And oh, how you want them to have an answer,
to throw a tantrum and walk out the door,
to say you can stick it, and that you'll be sorry,
or that they've finally got with the programme,
but the puffy hands, and the watery eyes,
and the vodka breath still sing their old song.
So you glance at the new guy from HR,
and he looks at you like you're holding a gun.
You plough on, still groping for easier words,
and again and again the same thing happens.
At the very moment you do the deed
they turn away slightly, exposing their neck,
like an antelope caught by some carnivore
on the merciless plains of the Masai Mara.
It's as if they had known it all along, still
carried some ancient mammalian imprint.
The spirit fails and they simply shut down,
the final surrender of the eternal victim.
You wait for them but there's nothing to say.
The hopelessness yawns, and the room is still.

Middleham's Crash

Spun out of his dreams, he would lie awake,
going over the day, playing back the dialogue:

how Ericsson had shamed him, publicly;
all the brilliant ripostes he had never made.

Singled out and marked like the painted bird,
he knew the others could peck him to death.

His appetite was gone. He was losing weight.
A little twitch appeared above his eyelid.

Ericsson, Ericsson, always bloody Ericsson;
his senseless cruelties, his arrogant demands.

And, yes, a part of him knew he was losing it
and sometimes he found he was talking to himself.

And then came the day he thought he was dying:
nausea, sweating, chest pains, and the shakes.

Just as he was fainting, Ericsson grabbed him,
dragged him outside and bent him over a rail.

Limply hanging there, staring at the pavement,
with Ericsson telling him he needed a holiday,

Middleham knew he'd arrived at the crossroads.
Wherever he went he would never be the same.

Soap

Jared warns Mary to stop playing games with Brendan, who's been driven to distraction by Jo at their meetings. Sonia and Phil nervously anticipate Justine's reaction while Callum discovers the truth about George, who's been getting some push-back from Geoff and Armando about the plan he's formulated with Susan. Meanwhile Theo takes Josh aside and gives him another talking-to just as Headquarters goes crazy, Sales goes into freefall, and all the phones start ringing at once. A call goes out to Andy, who's gone missing again, and Mark begins to see that leadership might not be the doddle he thought it was on the MBA. Ted's still trying to lose his virginity.

Bloody Politics

Says Mr Fox to Mr Donkey, *Can you take my meeting?*
Mr Donkey says, *Of course*, and promptly takes a beating.

Mr Lamb and Mr Owl saw Fox's power increased.
Mr Owl got his talons out — Mr Lamb got fleeced.

Mr Fox and Mr Lamb were both at the Leadership Lab.
Mr Fox became Chief Exec, Mr Lamb — kebab.

Some are clean and some are dirty; some are too pure to try.
If you want to change the world — do politics or die.

Note: This poem refers to a model of political skills created by Profs Simon
Baddeley and Kim James of Birmingham and Cranfield Universities which
liken manager's different attitudes towards politics to various animals — the
clever, cynical fox, wise owl, inept donkey and innocent lamb/sheep.

Conspirators

Cassius and Brutus in the Boardroom

By saying all is well we build a lie.
The last-but-one to speak holds all the pain.
There is an honest truth in a goodbye.

Who caused what bitter hurt, and when, and why,
Became the unvoiced note in our refrain.
By saying all was well we built a lie.

With power, good intentions ossify.
Our bitter words cracked bones with their disdain.
There is an honest truth in a goodbye.

The red-hot shame ensures that we comply,
Our inner hatreds spreading like a stain.
Yet, saying all is well, we build the lie.

We talk decorum but we still let fly,
And self-respect's a hard thing to regain.
There is at least some honour in goodbye.

And so we came to rocky Philippi,
To find our noble values had been slain.
By saying all was well we served the lie
And left ourselves no option but goodbye.

Alpha Male

Sometimes a subordinate gets too close,
says something you might not be ready for,
something too sharp, too dry to swallow.

From then on you're a raptor, watching,
wary of them and their subtle leverage.
They know, and knowing leaves them cowed.

Now and again, at a meeting or a function,
you catch them looking at you, sideways, scared.
You smile. They are grateful. It's a matter of time.

VI

The Jewel That You Need

Acorns and Angels

It is the lack we notice.
The crowded years of coffee-rush —
of back-to-back meetings and poker faces,
of sucking up and drilling down,
of saying yes when you really mean no —
all lead to a night in a nondescript room
above some anonymous, rain-soaked town.
You find yourself looking down at the traffic
crawling its way through the sodium glow.
You catch your reflection. You hear yourself
speaking: *I am not the person I wanted to be.*

If we are lucky we're granted a glimpse,
a grail-like vision of what a life can bring.
It changes you, stays with you, keeps you
hopeful — later it can even keep you sane.

Maybe you remember a summer's morning
when you were no more than a kid of fifteen.
You found yourself in ancient woodland
walking a path between stag-headed oaks.
Through an iron gate you came to a clearing
and in that moment you were changed.
You heard a sound like the beating of wings
and everything around you snapped into focus.
The pulsing connections between things
seemed clear to you, their subtlest workings
were lit from within; while above and below
and behind, you sensed a harmony, the deep
and moving music in the turning of the world.
It was as if you had burst through a barrier.
The acorn cracked and you started to grow.

Like a wound, that day travelled with you,
seemingly forgotten, but always there;
never grieved yet pined for, aching, itching,
haunting the days you surrendered to the city
as work and necessity carried you forward,
turning you into somebody else.
                                    I refuse
to live my life in exile from a better world,
thinking that I can find fulfilment
in someone else's hand-me-down dream.
I am going back to the wood — to the glade
and the green, to the morning light —
and I am going to search for the oak tree
that grew from the acorn while I was away.

What We Find at the Gates of Dawn

The soul is here to find its own way —
to do what's next, to experience.
Like a bird or a turtle, it cannot count,
it nurtures the small and squanders greatness.
Buttons are for pressing, doors to open —
especially those that say, *No Entry.*
A wall is a challenge, a cliff an invitation
to plunge a hundred feet into moonlit waters.
Feelings are food for a limitless hunger;
tears are drink, and anger seasoning.
To howl is to tremble the web of existence.
To laugh and to weep are to be most present.
What matters is beauty and authenticity —
the giggling twins at the bottom of the well.

Tao

Heaven and earth come first of all
And then individual things;
The sexes follow and then the bond
That love and affection brings.

Out of the bond the line is born
And out of the line respect —
We honour then the father first
Before the prince-elect.

Beneath these things mere law applies,
The rule of rank and caste,
And in such orders now ordained
Respect of right comes last.

So hold the tongue and cloak the eye
And, above all, still the mind —
In darkness let your spirit soar
As you suffer the rule of the blind.

Nel Mezzo del Cammin

For M W

In the middle of the journey of my life
I awoke to find myself in a dark wood.

Dante

And then, one day, you get another nudge.
It comes in a moment, an evocation —
mist on a meadow, the scent of narcissi,
the crunch and afterburn of radishes.

No one can say where this will take you.
All you can know is that everything will change.
Your road will dissolve, or fall away,
taking you down through an open trap-door
to the broken-glass places your earlier self
would have shied away from, instinctively.

Fierce eyes will loom out of the darkness,
scrawny old hands lay insistent claim;
wheedling questions will dog you like beggars,
old shames, like hangmen, stalk your dreams.

But in the dark wood, the bar room, or the pit,
you can find helpers and willing guides.
Strangers will befriend you, direct you upwards.
Rivals will gift you the one jewel that you need.

And slowly your path will unfold itself,
etched by starlight on a frosty night.
Oh, the stones will still be there —
this cold white track will never be generous,
never be kind — but a glimmer will show you

a way through the trees, and the moon
will be patient as you climb the mountain.
The dawn will bring you to a rosy summit
and you will have come to the view, the view.

The Mystery of Kindness

Almost on cue, at the end of their careers,
magically, as if fulfilling some final contract,
the masters — I mean the truly great artists —
seem to gravitate towards forgiveness.

Their styles become looser, their brushwork
more assured; they develop an economy
of line and gesture. It's as if they have come
to understand the world, and in doing so
have renounced the vanities of complexity —
settling in the end for the simplest of truths,
that what matters is kindness and compassion.

Mozart, at thirty-five, in the year of his death,
ignored and in debt, sick and close to madness,
manages to revisit the peak he climbed in Figaro
where the Countess forgives her errant husband;
only this time a clarinet and a string quartet,
warbling breathless at the edge of ecstasy,
are gathered in moments of heart-stopping beauty.
The sound, like a blessing, bathes us in love
of the world, and its folly, and everything we lose.

Beethoven in the grandeur of the last quartets,
the notes like fugitives stumbling in the dark;
or Rembrandt van Rijn, ruined and alone,
staring at himself in those final self-portraits:
lost and bewildered, dipping towards senility,
yet somehow triumphant in his humanity.

And Shakespeare — the mighty tragedies done
with Lear brought down to the quiet moment,
his one loving daughter dead in his arms —
forgives, but goes further: he gives up control.
Prospero, on his island, the vengeful mage,
his enemies reduced and his dreams accomplished,
forgives, from a place of unassailable power.

The detached and disembodied Ariel,
talking of the tearful lord Gonzalo, brings home
to his master the truth of his hardheartedness,
and so begins a process of redemption
by which the great, all-powerful sorcerer
breaks and then buries his tools of mastery,
renounces all thought of petty revenge
and with it the dominion he has over others.

What powers have we that we could give up?
What outdated dominance diminishes us?
Like the masters of old we could lighten our lives,
step into their knowing, their state of grace.
In pain and suffering they learned to be kind.
Maybe we, by forgiving, can come to forgiveness.

Dusk at the Château

This evening, alone, I waited for the night
as the water birds settled on the moat:
the cautious moorhen, the mallard and his drake,
the heron like a butler, poised and impeccable.
I watched the mayflies dancing on the water,
the heavy carp as they rose from the bottom,
rippling dark circles under the plane trees,
pooling out to a vast and empty stillness.

This is the nearest I get to my god — who speaks
to me in sound and scent — connecting me
to everything that has ever been or ever will be.

Sometimes I stand in awe of the world
as the colours drain from the end of the day,
and once I wept in the presence of beauty
knowing the poverty of my thin words —
but always, always I am refreshed,
and come away both strengthened and calmed,
when the god of the garden whispers to me,
telling me that I belong.

What He Really Meant to Say

Avoid regret.
Don't make excuses.
Live as if you had done no wrong.

Pay attention.
Be alive to the other.
Feel it quickening in all you see and do.

Practise descent.
Embrace the ecstatic.
Learn to give way to your curious soul.

Be gracious. Give.
Bless all who need a blessing.
Remember, your death is not your only debt.

Slow down. Stop.
Settle into the stillness.
Listen for the quiet at the heart of everything.

VII

Ericsson's Three-Sixty
What They Really Meant To Say

360 Degree Feedback is a common system of assessment used in organisations. Three-sixty refers to the 360 degrees of a circle – the individual assessed being figuratively in the centre. Feedback is provided by subordinates, peers, and superiors and is often deemed to be anonymous, though guarantees of anonymity are sometimes questioned.

Everyone carries a shadow, and the less it is embodied in the individual's conscious life, the blacker and denser it is.
Carl Gustav Jung

360° Feedback Number 1:
Self-Assessment

They may despise me but I'm still the best.
They all know I'm the one who saved the firm.
My numbers prove it — they're the acid test.
They may despise me but I'm still the best.
The others are just there to be finessed.
In meetings it's a joy to watch them squirm.
They may despise me but I'm still the best.
They all know I'm the one who'll lead the firm.

360° Feedback Number 2:
The Chairman

Maybe not the gentlest lad on the block
But then he's a man who can get things done.
His work in Spain caused one hell of a shock
Though he got a result, and we're number one.
He can shake things up. He's a fire fighter.
He's happy to drop things and get on a plane.
He wouldn't lay claim to a bishop's mitre
But who needs a nice-guy to put things in train.
That ugly business between him and Gray
Was a blip, a glitch, an aberration.
There's no bad feeling at the end of the day
And no one's thinking of a coronation.
He's useful, of course, I'd have him on the bus,
But not as the driver. He's not one of us.

360° Feedback Number 3:
The Peer Director

I sat there in the meeting yesterday
And as he spoke my flesh began to creep.
It wasn't so much what he had to say
As how he said it that was crass and cheap.
I know they think that HR's full of sheep
And not so much Resources as Remains
But what you scatter you will surely reap
And sanctioning abuse reaps hurricanes.
His way with women shows a lack of brains.
His language frankly shames the world of work.
He talks in terms of conquests and domains.
He's not a dinosaur, he's just a jerk.
He thinks he's got there, climbed the highest tree,
But he will pay for what he did to me.

360° Feedback Number 4:
The Direct Report

I like him. He's straight. He's one of the best.
It's good the way he calls a spade a spade.
He's not the kind of guy to get depressed.

He knows his stuff — as the figures attest.
He's sharp, decisive, never gets dismayed.
I like him. He's straight. He's one of the best.

That thing with Mary Gray — she's just obsessed.
It started as a joke he overplayed.
You pull a funny and they get distressed.

I've heard some women say that he's a pest.
If they would only try, I'm sure that they'd
quite like him. He's straight. He's one of the best.

Mind you, that chambermaid in Bucharest....
If he were a dog, I'd have had him spayed.
I kacked myself — he wasn't even stressed.

Our people there were really unimpressed.
Of course, he sorted it — saw she got paid.
That's like him. He's straight. He's one of the best
He's not the kind of guy to get depressed.

360° Feedback Number 5:
The Administrative Assistant

His smile is so disarming.
He always knows your name.
He's really very charming.
It's like he's playing a game.

He always knows your name.
He says he likes a natter.
It's like he's playing a game.
I know that I don't matter.

He said he'd like a natter.
He caught me by the loo.
I know that I don't matter.
I don't know what to do.

He pushed me in the loo.
He wouldn't let me go.
There's nothing I could do.
I wanted to say no.

He wouldn't let me go.
I've no one I can tell.
I wanted to say no.
It feels like I'm in hell.

I've no one I can tell.
My mum said, *Shut your gob.*
It feels like I'm in hell.
But a job's a job's a job.

So I will shut my gob.
And no one has to know.
And I will do my job.
I've nowhere else to go.

And no one here will know
Because he's very charming.
I've nowhere else to go.
His smile was so disarming.

360° Feedback Number 6:
The Management Services Co-ordinator

Sharon said he's a lovely boss
So I got him a Christmas gift.
It's not the kind of thing he wears
But he winked at me in the lift.

Sharon said to change my look,
Said he thinks I'm too arty-farty.
Well, he may not like my new tattoo
But he grabbed me at the party.

Sharon says I should leave him be,
Says not to queer her pitch.
But I'm the one with the Gucci bag.
And he's the one with the itch.

Can't say I like the job that much
And that Sharon makes me sick.
But a girl's gotta do what a girl's gotta do
When her boss thinks with his dick.

360° Feedback Number 7:
The Chief Executive

What do you do with a damaged winner,
One who has got all the skills and the drive;
One who can draw up a plan over dinner,
keep the markets happy, and the firm alive?
I've tried to stay blind to the odd transgression,
Treated him as if he were the chosen son,
But now it's a matter of my succession.
My dream could be shredded before it's begun.
This thing with Mary, this rift in the lute,
Was wrong; he needed to keep her on side.
She's ruthless. She's pushy. A boardroom dispute
Could see him exposed — he'd be crucified.
It's about reputation, not about clout.
He's not worth the trouble. He's a fool. He's out.

VIII

The Long Black Bag

An Away-Day with the Shadow

Under the trees the chestnut cattle
are munching slow bunches of sweet young spring.
The heron is pretending to be invisible
and mayflies glitter in the sycamore shade.

Who'd have thought that ill could thrive here
and yet it does — in every one of us.
That kind and supportive manager over there
is eating her young team: gnawing their bones,
sucking out the marrow, destroying their chances
with her relentless care and devouring nurture.
That brilliant enthusiast, jumping up and down,
with fifteen solutions and a redesign for breakfast,
is sending his colleagues into spirals of despair,
firing off ideas like a Catherine wheel, never allowing
any one thing the time it needs to settle or grow.
The mean-lipped man, sitting in the corner, who's
been there, done that, seen it fail a thousand times,
who knows a dozen creative ways to strangle an idea,
is poisoning the company he professes to love
with his cynical bile and his fear of change.
And I, who worked my way up from nothing,
who built a career out of ashtrays and beer-mats,
gaming chips and coffee cups, nightshifts and overtime;
who worked all the hours the gods of money sent,
who hit my targets year on year — I have stood
in a London street as one of my team, my chosen crew,
dropped his gaze and walked right past me,
too ashamed to look me in the eye:
afraid of the tyrant that he was working for,
afraid of the bully that I had become....

A slow carp stirs the lazy water. A moorhen putters.
The mallard shepherds her two remaining chicks.
Somewhere in the depths the great pike is stirring.
The water birds pretend he isn't there.

And on the Seventh Day

God knows, it's easy enough to point the finger.
We're all churchwardens when we read the papers.
Disgust and self-righteousness are par for the course
on a slow suburban Sunday morning.
       But at night,
when the tomcats of loneliness call, and things
that live on secrets stretch themselves and stir,
dapper little accountants from Wimbledon
reach for the phone with a trembling hand
to whisper obscenities to part-time women
who yawn as they do it for them — do it all night.
Then salesmen, surveyors and warehousemen,
plasterers and clerks and the occasional priest,
the meek and the mild and the simply ordinary,
step into the neon-twisted light, blinking
and gulping and slowly transforming themselves
into leather-clad predators or hungry-angry lads.
Then the Chairman, the Chief, the public man
waits in his car at the edge of the Common,
or walks among the silent, cruising shadows,
risking the world for a moment of excitement,
for a buzz that his daylight self can't allow.
And somewhere in the bushes, with his heart
in his mouth, stands a man whom we nod to
or smile at in the supermarket. And he's scared
and excited and feeling foolish as he waits there,
naked but for a raincoat. And he's not too sure
why he's there again, or why the siren voices
should have brought him back. But he's back
and he's driven to show himself to a woman
who may scream when she sees what he is doing,
or hurry by in shame, or call for the police.

And the rest of him will sit on Sunday morning,
flicking through the usual spread of crucifixions.
And once again he'll feel that little pang of envy
when he reads about the sinners who can rest.

Between Dream and Action

And who betrayed you?
Who rose up darkly between dream and action
to comfort and stab with equal aplomb?

Did you see the signs?
Did you read the language, of eyebrow and shoulder,
of significant look and dismissive wave,
the unwitting giveaway in a shrug or a sneer,
the dull lizard eyes behind a smile?

Or was it you who betrayed yourself
with your restless hunger and second-hand certainties?
Maybe you were ambushed by your need to be loved,
or your seeping-cynical view of the world?

What betrays us is the insistent past
which demands that we play out its family fugue —
statement, restatement, in endless repetition,
parlaying a wound into a way of life.

The past, we can be sure, plays both major and minor.
We may not choose to notice, but it's always there.

Signs and Omens

After the acquisitions,
when they were Number One,
when the CEO was sanctified
and the City stood in awe
of the sheer glass building
and the breathtaking results;

when the board no longer
spoke with funny accents
and no one remembered
the pokey little workshop
full of spanners and smells
where it all began;

at the very moment they
all stopped eating together;

when their lives were polished
and their lawns neatly mown,
their untidy wives repackaged
and put on the programme;
when their sons no longer
went away to war —

the Chairman awoke,
screaming in the night,
chased from his dreams
by tearing beaks and talons.
Everyone agreed he was
overworked, exhausted.
Somehow no one noticed
the claw marks on the door.

The Weight of Others' Grief

Home from working at a corporate university —
five days spent with a dozen executives,
kind, decent people, eager to achieve,
yet strangers to their darkling inner lives.
In my garden the evening swirls with swallows,
a nuthatch clings to the mortar of a wall,
collared doves announce their comforting presence,
while somewhere above the climbing rose,
hidden in the beech, an early mistle thrush
begins his wild, ecstatic evensong.
I stand for a while with my back to the house.
Breathing in the stillness, I burst into tears.

IX

In Time of Darkness

Sifting the Silence

Say a little prayer for the friends you've lost,
the ones who shied away from friendship,
calling you weak for being kind,
and the ones you pushed away yourself,
playing the hero in a movie called The Job.

A hero has few enough buddies at thirty.
Work kills trust and sometimes kills a friend.
The roaring pack of endless youth
becomes a thoughtful, mortal band,
decimated by failure and fear in competition.

At thirty-five you're down to ones and twos.
You tell yourselves the prize is worth it
and ignore the signs that say 'Beware'.
You get your head down, redouble your efforts,
and soon you're entering heart-attack country.

You turn up shocked at a couple of funerals
and then you're forty, and alone.
That's when you start spilling your guts out,
pissed, in pubs, to uninterested strangers
or in bed to women who quickly grow tired
of carrying yet another man's pain.

Your body is tense. You long to be held
but nobody touches you because you're in charge.
So you sit in your office, sifting the silence,
and sometimes at night you think about calling
one of the fellas who fell off the wire.

Cometh the Hour

Then comes the day that calls for something else,
the day you couldn't have trained for
or been warned about. E-mails flutter down
like autumn leaves, each one a brittle separation.

People begin to look at you differently —
sideways, expectant, needing you to lead them;
the banter shrivels and the check-ins wither;
offices and corridors fill with drifts of silence.

This is the day that you have been waiting for,
the single defining moment of your life.
Looking back, everything points to today;
the scene has been set for triumph, or disaster.

It's two o'clock in the morning, and you are awake,
the weight of your loneliness pressing down.
The voices gather and the doubts collect —
your whole world trembles as the question is asked.

Clink

This is how we meet ourselves:
at night, alone, walking empty rooms;
the rattle of ice in a crystal glass,
the glug of Scotch, the ice complaining;
the late-night radio's easy comfort
dwindling into frozen silence. Clink.

This is when the voices come:
hissing, insistent, out of the dark
and terrible room we never inspect
unless we have to. You're a fraud,
a failure. They've found you out.
You're a wastrel. Worthless! Clink.

This is when our hopes congeal,
curdle in the glare of numbers,
desiccate and fall away, taking
friends and loved ones with them.
Red-eyed, staring, we're left to brood
upon the certain cause, the link.

For this is when the paper trail
of metrics, profiles and appraisals,
hints and outbursts, resignations,
leads us back to our midnight office
where we find the same indictment
signed by everyone we knew. Clink.

This is when the lights go out
the system fails, and the candles gutter.
In the darkness no one knows you;
wealth and status count for nothing.
This is when the power ebbs. You lose
your edge. You're the first to blink.

So this is where we find ourselves
in the middle of our own dark night,
facing the path of voices and choices
that leads us to the cold hard dawn.
Do we meet the unforgiving moment?
Do we grow or do we shrink? Clink.

Middleham's Task List

It never quite happened: my one-day-some-day,
never-never dream. I tick every box. I'm Mr Reliable,
yet somehow my ambitions have melted away.

Presentation. E-mails. Meeting with Cybertec.

Once I believed that I could take on the world,
but my mind and my body started letting me down.
Now, when the bathroom mirror sneaks up on me,
I don't see my potential, I see grey hair.

Spreadsheets. Projections. Breakdown for Ericsson.

My promising, shiny, white-collar life has shrunk
to a house and a BMW, fantasy novels on the beach,
and a wife who's got a problem with reality.

Set up three-sixties. Marketing strategy.

It began with odd items that twisted themselves
into tearful scenes, and confessions about shoplifting.
I wanted to help but I couldn't find the words.

Budget meeting with Mergers and Acquisitions.

We were beautiful once, standing on our hilltop,
holding each other with everything before us;
mapped out and waiting, ours for the taking.

Annual returns to Companies House.
Auditors. Accountants. Away-day lunch.

Sometimes I want to shout 'I did all this for you!'
though she'd only shout back 'I never wanted it'.
And so we spend our evenings in silence ...

Report to the Board. Get back to Robinson.
Think about getting another upgrade.

A Loss

He looks in the mirror,
at the hard grey eyes,
and sees that he has
lost his humility.
The first-class check-in
and the patient limo
have robbed him
of his one true talent,
an ability to be less-than
yet undiminished.

The Taoist sages speak
of Chien, the holy quality
of modesty. What is lowly,
they say, is lifted up —
what is great is decreased,
worn down, brought low.

He senses a change
in the emptying of years,
a weight that settles
round his solitary heart.
He thinks of his properties,
his balanced portfolio,
his polished collections
of beautiful things,
and, with a grunt, accepts
that he will die, wealthy,
respected, and alone.

A Four-O'Clock-in-the-Morning Poem

The air is heavy with the threat of thunder:
slow, thick, muggy, oppressive.

He has never been so lonely —
standing there in the darkness, on the path,
unsure about whether to turn or go on.
This is his time for being alone,
for answering the questions
that have always plagued him,
for meeting the doubts and shaming imperatives,
the cruel and punishing inner voices
that say, *You shouldn't. You can't. You won't.*

Somewhere in the dark his dream lies diminished,
reduced to a tiny, guttering hope.
For the moment he survives on faith,
faith in himself, in his courage and resilience;
his in-built ability to meet the voices,
endure them, confront them, face them down —
though even that lies in the balance.

Four o'clock now — the time at which the old defences
fail to serve and fall away.
He sees a thin, faint light up ahead.
He makes his choice, and moves towards it.

The Winner

To succeed, he checked out years ago,
went missing — like you do.
Grabbed a couple of comforting notions,
packed some prejudices and did a runner.
Left his body — like you do.

Filled the hole with coffee and smokes,
a few drinks at lunchtime — like you do.
Then later a few between six and the close.
There's nowhere to go and you daren't go home.
Best to get high again — like you do.

Left his body but the ache remained.
Tried to work around it — like you do.
Tried to explain when she threatened to leave.
Threatened her back, said he'd fight to the end.
Waved as she drove away — like you do.

Saw that he'd lost himself years ago.
Tried to get sorted — like you do.
Cleaned himself up and got back into action
but the trap-door opened and he fell through.
That's when he fell apart — like you do.

The Sacrifice

Hard-arsed, elegant, frighteningly competent,
she's made her way to the top, or near it.
Nails perfect, very little make-up,
hair bobbed shorter than she'd like it to be,
She's got there, she's a player,
a woman to be reckoned with, a woman
who's had to prove herself better than any man.
And now, in her forties, it's beginning to tell.
The deal that she struck
with the stranger at the cross-roads —
or was it at that conference when she was twenty-five —
became an invoice, a reminder, and finally a summons.
Called, like Abraham, she's sacrificed her children
though Mammon, unlike Jehovah, rarely stays the hand.
Home after bedtime and missing the odd sports day
became a distance, and a silence at the end of the phone.
Love is a thing that you do at the weekends:
a chequebook, a buy-out, a thing of the past.

Middleham's Howl

What's madness but nobility of soul
At odds with circumstance? The day's on fire!

Theodore Roethke

I want the office ceiling to burst open
and the SAS to come abseiling down.
I want a message to arrive from Mogadishu
where pirates are besieging my tattooed friend
who's waiting for me with a revved-up powerboat,
a bag full of diamonds, and a song in his heart.
There's a code and a key, and a hurried letter
that says only I can save him now —
that the answer lies in a strongbox in Zurich,
and that I should get myself to the airport.

Alternatively I could settle for Ericsson,
going up like a rocket and finally exploding,
whining and shrieking in a whizz-bang cluster
of puffball, magenta and yellow fireworks.

I want to be kidnapped, or wake up elsewhere,
to become a detective, or blow the whistle.
I want to grow my hair and fool them all
into thinking I'm weak — when, in my blindness,
I can stand, and push, and pull at the pillars
till their empty temple comes tumbling down.

Failing that, I'd settle for a full week's sanity
with bubbles popping and the stables cleansed.
I want to stop pretending that all is well,
to give up the mantra of 'business as usual';

and I want my children to imagine a future
beyond a churning treadmill of debt.
                              Oh yes,
and I want someone to tell me, honestly
why it had to come down to this: the grind,
the hours, the lack of a purpose, the linked-in,
networked boundlessness of everything;
the loss of my honour, the loss of my family,
the loss of belonging, and the loss of belief.

Risk Assessment

The hole in your heart begins with a sigh
or a tiny rip of consenting silence.
Your eyes look down, your throat constricts
when the man at the meeting, says,
Any Questions?
                    Later you hear yourself
using his words. The rip opens up a little
but what you feel is your voice sitting
differently in your mouth. This new dry
language has a sharp metallic aftertaste
but you can't help thinking it's kind of sexy.
There's something about it makes you feel
powerful.
                    Over time you come to spot
an emptiness where once there was feeling.
The work still feeds you — up to a point —
but your joy, your compassion, your ability
to love has bled out through the ragged
aperture that now gapes open every night.

You fill the hole with sex or with chocolate;
you drink, you gamble, you take a bit of spliff,
but most days it's the work that medicates.
You begin to pretend there is no hole.

They feel it at home — this closing down —
and friends stop calling because you're so busy.
You argue, you win, you get your own way.
You get a reputation and people avoid you.
If you are lucky a loved one speaks up, says
they've had enough of your walls and barriers.
You spend angry nights of resentful repair,
stitching up the hole with the threads of loss.
Otherwise you work on — your hollow heart

echoing to the sounds of remembered closeness,
looking forward to a windswept retirement,
and a gravestone that says, *He did his job.*

Trois Leçons de Ténèbres

The voices spiral up into the night,
mezzo and soprano joined in sadness,
the Hebrew letters of the Jeremiad
framing the opening of a troubled heart.
Music written for a dying king.

He has come to the time of ashes.
Nothing could have prepared him for this.
Like the dying Louis, he sees his surroundings
as a gilded prison confining his soul.
The face in the director's washroom mirror
is greyer and older by a decade, etched
with lines born of worry, not laughter.
The shoulders sag with the weight of lives
dependent on his every decision.
His eyes are wary, watchful, and reserved
like an old master's portrait, full of doubt.

This is not what I signed up to.

Back in his wood-and-leather-scented office
he looks down on the corporate plaza below
where a solitary figure is gazing up
at his silhouette, framed in the last lit window.
For a fleeting moment their eyes seem to meet,
each one envying the other's imagined freedom.
Then the man below raises his fist
in an ancient gesture of impotent defiance —
and in this moment, seven floors above him,
another king comes to understand loneliness.

Note: The three lessons of Tenebrae (Holy Week) were written for King Louis XIV by his court composer, François Couperin (1668-1733) and performed by nuns as he lay dying. The music is considered to be amongst the most exquisite of the Baroque.

X

Back to the Garden

The Travelling Soul

After the thunder and the rain,
the sudden squall which broke the evening,
morning comes with its quiet blessing
of dappled stillness and steaming sunlight.

The graceful ash trees slowly exhale,
songbirds return to their confident foraging,
an ancient church bell calls the hour
and the new day opens like a bud.

I have ached to stand in such quiet moments,
my senses alive to every happening:
the drilling of the woodpecker,
the rootlings of the boar,
the delicate twitch of the grazing deer.

I want the smell of the grass to heal me,
the dew to cleanse my travelling soul.
This morning I can be a part of the stillness.
Today I can rest in the calm of the world.

The Old Hut in the Woods

He's been away too long. The desire
for an outcome and the search for an edge
have kept him from the enchanted circle
where he found himself all those years ago.

He's a stranger now to those who met him:
the sad-eyed elders with their open hearts,
the wild yet gentle story-makers
who offered help, and hearth, and hearing.

He's acquired much, yet given himself away,
naive in spite of his practised modernity.
His credit is blown. His capital's exhausted.
His waxy wings lie broken on the ground.

Ever reluctant to own a mistake,
a part of him hankers for business as usual.
But something has changed. He is older now,
no longer so certain of his models and plans.

The tumbledown hut is in need of an airing.
The fire has gone out and the ashes are cold.
Yearning for the past yet facing the future,
he enters the gloom, and begins to light a fire.

Middleham's Pilgrimage

*Do you not see how necessary a world of pains and troubles is
to school an intelligence and make it a soul?*

John Keats

First, in a quiet moment, he noticed
the sweetness in the huddle of women
gathered round the intern who was crying;
how their faces were softened by soothing her,
how the half-worded, cooing noises they made
and their gentle, tentative stroking gestures
filled the office with the perfume of kindness.
Next the aroma sent him spinning back
to a place where he was a child being sung to
by a woman who was dressing a cut
that he'd brought to her through summer tears.
He felt once again her elderly hands
cupping his face and cooling his skin;
remembered the look in her widow's eyes —
half hurt, half care, and a third half tenderness —
as she solemnly kissed him on the forehead,
loving the boy for the men who were gone.

From then on they seemed to be everywhere,
silent reminders and phantom fragrances,
speaking to him of kindness and gentleness
in his sharp-edged, metallic, masculine world.
His voice changed, sounded deeper in his chest,
and he knew he wanted to reach out and touch
people — not in a needy or controlling way
but as a new found way of being human.

Slowly the petrified child came to life,
swam free in his dreams and came to the surface;
smiling, chuckling, weeping at stories,
alive in a way he could hardly remember.

And somewhere the old woman's voice repeated
a mantra he couldn't remember her saying.
Love's not a piece of Victoria sponge —
giving it away doesn't mean you lose it.

And that was when Jill had her little seizure,
before the doctors had diagnosed her illness.
She was sitting in the meeting looking blank
when suddenly she was shaking and muttering.
Jackson was alarmed, called for a first-aider,
the room was emptying, people were scared,
even though she was regaining consciousness.

And that was how Middleham came home.
He stood and went to her, called her by name,
noting her distress at her loss of control.
Gently he wrapped her in his arms, whispered
that everything was going to be okay, cleared
the room and simply held her, let her weep
on his chest to bury her embarrassment.
Slowly she gathered and looked up at him
as the others fussed back into the room.
I never thought you could be so kind, she said.
Neither did I, said Middleham. *Thank you.*

Other Voices

The roses say it — in their pinkness —
cheerful little sages, nodding against a wall;

the jackdaws chuckling in the treetops,
the woodpecker yaffling across the lawn.

The swallow calls to you, slicing the air;
the humble robin, the fierce little wren.

The linden heavy with her sticky chrism,
the whispering chestnut and the graceful ash;

the grass, the weeds, the stones themselves —
silent yet conversing, deeply connected —

Everything watching, everything waiting,
Welcoming you to this beginning.

In Praise of Pottering

I've set today aside for pottering,
for giving my rock-rolling Sisyphus a rest.
It's not that I dislike work, I love it,
now that I've married my work to my calling,
but pottering feeds a different part of me:
the unanticipated silliness of it,
the aimless, unmeasured, undecided joy
of timing, planning, and arranging nothing.
I think I'll wander down to the orchard.
Maybe sit on the old stone cider-press,
or visit the briar patch that, for a year or so,
has blocked the way down to the creek.
I should have dealt with that briar by now...
You see!
The rock rolls back to the foot of the hill
and dusty, grunting Sisyphus
just has to turn it into a project.
No. Today my job is to do no job;
to float in idleness like the duckweed
that I might find if I got down to the water.
It's not my job to do today,
but simply to be in the pottering moment:
not to struggle, not to endeavour,
not to organize, not to fix,
not to strive, not even to create;
but merely to witness, to observe, to see,
to be present to the glory of this ordinary day.

A Challenge

Did you ever get up in the muddle before dawn
for no better reason than that you wanted
to greet the sunrise?
Did you ever dress quietly, with serious intent,
and pick your way over wintry fields
to arrive at a place that you once imagined
bathed in the first clear light of morning?
And did you wait as the dawning grew,
moved through purple, to mauve, to grey,
from excitement to boredom, to a kind of calm
as you gently noticed your insignificance?
And did you mutter unfamiliar words
that seemed to come from somewhere else,
ancient words of dread and devotion,
words of welcome and astonishment?
And when at last the tired sun
issued from the earth like a molten copper head,
did you notice the hawk that flew at you,
rose in a way that made everything sacred,
stooped in a way that made the day blaze?

Or did you sleepwalk into the morning,
bending your dreams to another's purpose,
listening to the news, half hoping for a cataclysm,
anything to make the tired day more real.

Slowed

Travelling homeward, another week done —
mobile muttering in my pocket,
mind on the next twenty things I need to do —
I'm caught by a shaft of evening sunlight.

It often happens on this stretch of line:
crimson light spilling over the embankment
as the seven-fifteen from Paddington
stretches out into Berkshire and Wiltshire.

I've been irritated by this in the past;
pulled down the blind when across the aisle,
frowned in impotence where I'm sitting now —
yet somehow today I'm ripe to be slowed.

Feeling the sun still strong on my face,
I lay my head back against my seat.
A tired world reddens beneath my eyelids
till we gradually curve round into shade.

I loll and rest my head against the window,
feeling the pull and push of the engines.
The landscape slides by, gently evolving,
red brick and tile giving way to stone.

I trace the distant line of the downs,
gently caress the long spine of history:
tumuli, hill forts, the White Horse at Uffington,
the tump of beeches that shades Wayland's Smithy.

The train powers on, carrying me westward.
The long day dims and the landscape fades.
I realise how much I've come to love this country;
love its flinty soil, love its very bones.

XI

Not Yet Ithaca

Hitting the Straight

For M B

It's not that I'm old,
I'm just hitting the straight,
but I'm aware this morning,
I mean bodily aware,
that death has remembered
its home in my bones,
the little dot of Yin
in the paisley-curl of my Yang,
and that it's stirring,
worming, waiting to collect.
Sometimes I'm so tired
I could let it embrace me…
but, you know how it is,
the woodpigeon's working
on its irritating call
and the swifts are plying
the sky above the city.
I rise and turn towards
the day and its action,
pulled by the old,
demanding machinery
that will not,
cannot, let me let go.

The Garden on the Island

It is autumn in the Jardin de l'Île.
The plane trees are dying again,
offering up their splendour. Their leaves
flutter gently, carpeting the moat
where the great pike moves
through deep forgetful water,
knowing exactly what he needs to do.
The sun dips into the ivy-strangled oaks
and another brave cycle comes to an end.

I have been happy here — good work
among friends, some time for reflection,
a few quiet words strung hopefully together —
though beyond the water, in the busy world,
death, like the pike, has been making his move:
stealthily, inexorably, shockingly greedy,
his sudden jaws appearing from nowhere.

The owls are calling along the avenue.
Soon they'll be quartering the well-cropped grass.
Alone now, I am thinking of W. B. Yeats,
of beauty and terror and the paradox of age.
I am learning to live in the presence of death,
yet somehow still opening to the rapture of life.
I stand at my window and breathe in the evening.
The pike settles down in the deep dark mud.

Middleham's Last Hurrah

Meetings don't crackle in the way they used to.
His eyes, long dulled by recycled dreams,
sit back in a face as crumpled as his suit.
He's been there, done that, bought three visions,
defended them piecemeal, and watched them die
as the winds of fashion and leadership changed.

He's taken the knocks, come back for more,
carried the can and done other's dirty work.
Now you would say he was looking downhill,
on the slow descent to a corporate farewell;
schmoozing a transfer to a gentler post —
Paris or Rome, the Brussels Office, Swindon.

But you'd be wrong to think it was over.
Like Odysseus, he knows he's blown his return.
The sound of the water lapping at the dock,
the wind in the woodwork, and the screech of gulls
echo down the bland grey plastic corridors,
calling to him through the air conditioning.

There's some adventure still wants to happen,
some further demand that needs to be answered;
some deed, some challenge, some rich descent
that speaks to the soul he's compromised.
For yes, it's his soul that needs to be fed now,
needs to be dusted down, watered and freed.

Come on, fellas, let's see what can be done
when sad old geezers stir their wrinkled butts.
It's never too late to re-engage the heart,
to come at the passion we turned our backs on.
The days grow shorter and the nights are cold.
We can see what's coming, but why surrender?

Who knows what griefs may yet befall us?
Who knows what indignities lie in wait?
We may be thought of as yesterday's fools
and mocked by those who have yet to fail,
but we still have the maps of our ambition.
There's something in us still wants to be lived.

Home from the Office and Checking his E-mails, He is Visited by his Ageing Cat

Worn-out old cat, crouched by his laptop,
breathing laboured, not long for this world;

fierce little organism, hanging on in there,
still keen to hunt, to make another kill,

but settling for touch and a gentle voice,
an arm to rest against, a familiar warmth.

Her once-sleek fur is tatty and unkempt,
her purring erratic in her lattice of bones.

He wants to help her, to make it easier,
but his world is calling, with its demands.

He knows this may be their last time together:
unnoted, undiarised, unspoken of to anyone.

So he stays with her, quietly doing his e-mails,
fulfilling the offices of death and friendship.

In My Fiftieth Year

October had me thinking about dying.
The specialist had dropped a few new words
into my humdrum, day-to-day vocabulary,
sharp, angular words like prostate, blood test and tumour.
I waited as the days grew shorter, burned faster,
turning for consolation to Alden Nowlan and Raymond Carver,
poets who both died conscious at fifty,
facing the implacable mugger that is cancer.

Alden got there by main strength and character,
eyeball to eyeball with the merciless thug,
managing to raise a modicum of grace
at each new threat and ugly demand.
Ray was something else. He'd made the journey,
had travelled to despair and way beyond.
He knew that his life, or what he had left of it,
was a gift over which he had neither right nor dominion.
In fact, he renounced all pretence to control
and settled for the astonishing beauty of the moment.

Having seen the mugger's shadow in the alleyway,
having heard the click of his approaching heels,
I've watched him, in his irrational way
move on, seeking someone else to terrorise.
Whatever comes now, I think I'm ready.
My life, like Carver's, has become a boon.
For me, each day's an unexpected benison,
a deepening I never thought to witness.
I'm privileged to see beauty and to know what I'm seeing,
to recognise love in its glory and variety.
I have a place where my heart can gather itself.
I have friends and the goodwill of my dead.
In my fiftieth year I have come in to land —
rich in love and beauty I am truly blessed.

Cool Hands and a Blessing

In Memoriam James Hillman

I was thinking of James Hillman,
of how he loved a word, and I remembered
the afternoon he talked about yearning:
singled it out as an old English usage,
a word he rarely heard back home
where 'needs' are talked about,
and 'getting what you want', but where
the soul's desire, and the deeper longings,
are left unspoken — to charge the air.

I was struck by the way he sat with the word,
savoured it, rolled it around his mouth.
Yearning. Yearning. What is it you yearn for?
and the quiet ripple that ran around the room
lapped at the hearts of a hundred men and women,
spoke to the unlived, unfulfilled parts of us,
the giants in us who never were,
the sibyls and the prophets, the fearless
explorers who never found their ocean,
nor a Northwest Passage through the icy wastes,
who never said goodbye to a stifling town
with their eyes alight and their blood atingle,
nor stood at last above a sleepy village
they had longed for through the wildest nights;
the kindly remembered voices calling,
All is forgiven. You can come home now.

Yearning - we're both called and driven by it,
even when we don't know what it is:
for fame, for absolution, for acquittal,
for the lost and forgotten laughter of youth,
for love, for touch, for a simple kindness,
for the cool dry hands and the silent blessings
of the ones that we loved, who are no more.

Elderhood

I am no longer your leader, your boss.
My scrip of power over you —
such as it was — no longer holds.
I've ceased to be your imagined father.
Like a pilgrim or a mendicant, I have moved on.
I have no right to inhabit your dreams,
to loom like a shadow on your patch of sunlight.
Likewise you must let me go;
see me stumble if I must, see me falter and fail.

Giving up the keys was never going to be easy.
Surrendering the seal meant a deal of loss.
In my case it took me down, and down,
layer by layer, to the heart of the onion,
to the place where there seems to be no self,
where we are most naked, most alone.
What I found there, stripped, was a beginning.
The parting with power was a shedding of skins.
The sense of the cool, sharp wind on my flesh
was a moment recalled from a long-forgotten rite.

I am different now — and so are you.
What I ask of you is that you see me so:
not a wielder of power, no longer a player,
not a man who would choose to make or mar,
but a wilder, less demanding traveller,
one who's relinquished the need to compete.
Know me. See me. Forgive me my changes,
They will happen to you. There's a long way to go.

XII

Epilogue

Out There

There's a kid out there with something to say
who is being stopped from saying it.
Life has put a gag in her mouth —
as cruel as a kidnapper's calloused hand.
Some schoolyard fear, some imagined dread,
some all-too-real and paralysing shame
leaves her diminished and pigeon-toed,
staring at the floor in abject silence.

I want to remove that suffocating rag
and lead her out to a place of safety,
a place where her voice can find its wings,
where she can talk, and learn to sing.
I want to be there, with everyone watching,
on the day that she finally speaks her truth,
and I want them to hear what she has to say,
because she is a woman who can change the world.

About the Author

William Ayot worked in London's gaming industry while developing as a writer and studying personal development. He was a co-founding director of Olivier Mythodrama, a groundbreaking creative consultancy, which teaches leadership through myth, poetry and theatre practise. Global clients have included blue chip corporations, ministries, NGOs and some of the world's top business schools. William recently reduced his business commitments to concentrate on setting up NaCOT (National Centre for the Oral Tradition), a visionary project devoted to creating the UK's first dedicated home for the oral tradition which includes poetry, storytelling, comedy, oratory and public speaking of all kinds. William still works with a limited number of clients, as a keynote speaker, leadership coach and poet-in-residence. His poems are increasingly well know in the business community, appearing on the web, and in books such as *The X & Y of Leadership* (Spiro), *Trust Matters* (Jossey Bass), *Discovery* (Cyan-Marshall Cavendish), *Leading from Within* (Jossey Bass), and *Into the Further Reaches* (PS Avalon). William lives with his wife, Juliet Grayson Ayot in a restored Monmouthshire Gentry House near Chepstow, South-East Wales.

Apart from charting the inner journey of leadership, William Ayot has also written movingly and powerfully about his descent into, and return from, the underworld of self-discovery and personal development. Follow this inspiring journey in *The Inheritance*, also published by PS Avalon.

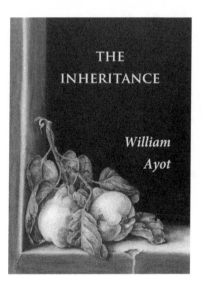

"William Ayot's poems are wrung out of necessity, the terrible inheritance that had to be told. The poems speak with a fine control and intensity. His performance takes this control to a different level. Pitch-perfect, he faces up to 'the dogs of disaster' with wit and compassion, a glass raised against the darkness ..." *Imtiaz Dharker*

CPSIA information can be obtained
at www.ICGtesting.com
Printed in the USA
BVHW03s2331280318
511827BV00008B/901/P